LEGENDARY LIVES

Dolly Parton

by Betsy Rathburn
Illustrated by
Claudia Marianno

BLASTOFF! MISSIONS

BLASTOFF! MISSIONS, AN IMPRINT OF
BELLWETHER MEDIA BY FLUTTERBEE

Blastoff! Missions takes you on a learning adventure! Colorful illustrations and exciting narratives highlight cool facts about our world and beyond. Read the mission goals and follow the narrative to gain knowledge, build reading skills, and have fun!

Traditional Nonfiction

Narrative Nonfiction

Blastoff! Universe

MISSION GOALS

- FIND YOUR SIGHT WORDS IN THE BOOK.
- LEARN MORE ABOUT DOLLY PARTON'S LIFE.
- LEARN HOW DOLLY PARTON BECAME A COUNTRY MUSIC STAR.

This edition first published in 2026 by Bellwether Media, Inc.

For information regarding permission, write to Bellwether Media, Inc., Attention: Permissions Department, 3500 American Blvd W, Suite 150, Bloomington, MN 55431.

Library of Congress Cataloging-in-Publication Data is available at www.loc.gov or upon request from the publisher.

ISBN: 9798893048438 (hardcover)
ISBN: 9798898800178 (paperback)
ISBN: 9798893049435 (ebook)

Editor: Rebecca Sabelko Designer: Andrea Schneider

Printed in the United States of America, North Mankato, MN.

This is **Blastoff Jimmy**! He is here to help you on your mission and share fun facts along the way!

Table of Contents

Country Queen

Dolly Parton steps onto the stage. She **strums** a guitar. She sings a song about her childhood in the Smoky Mountains.

The crowd loves Dolly's country music!

Rising Star

Dolly is seven years old. She lives with her family in Tennessee.

JIMMY SAYS

Dolly had 11 brothers and sisters. They lived with their parents in a two-room log cabin.

She loves music. She sings and plays a homemade guitar. She made it from an old **mandolin**.

Dolly is 11 years old. She has been writing songs for about six years. She often sings on television.

Today, she makes her first recording. It is called "Puppy Love."

Porter Wagoner
award

It is 1968. Dolly is a regular on *The Porter Wagoner Show.*

Today, she wins a big award. She and Porter are honored as the Vocal Group of the Year!

The Porter
Wagoner Show

JIMMY SAYS

"I Will Always Love You" is another hit song from Dolly's solo album. Whitney Houston recorded a version in 1992. This version became even more famous than Dolly's!

Dolly has released her 13th **solo** album. Its first **single** is "Jolene." She performs it on *The Porter Wagoner Show*.

The song tops country music charts!

Dolly stars in her first movie. It is called *9 to 5*. Dolly wrote the movie's main song!

She wins Grammy Awards for the song in 1982.

Beyond Music

Dollywood

It is 1986. A crowd gathers in Pigeon Forge, Tennessee. Today is the grand opening of Dollywood!

Dolly welcomes guests to her new **theme park**.

It is 1995. Dolly has a new idea. She wants kids to discover the magic of reading.

She starts Imagination Library. It gives free books to kids every month!

JIMMY SAYS

Imagination Library has given away more than 270 million free books to children!

A Music Legend

Tonight, Dolly is being honored. She will be added to the Rock and Roll Hall of Fame.

She performs "Jolene" with other famous musicians. She is a music **legend**!

Dolly Parton Profile

Born

January 19, 1946, in Locust Ridge, Tennessee

Accomplishments

A country music artist who has written thousands of songs and given away millions of books

Timeline

1967: appears on *The Porter Wagoner Show* for the first time

1973: releases "Jolene" and "I Will Always Love You" on the album *Jolene*

1980: stars in her first movie, *9 to 5*

1986: opens the Dollywood theme park

1995: starts Imagination Library to give books to kids

2022: is added to the Rock and Roll Hall of Fame

Glossary

legend–a person who is well known for something

mandolin–a musical instrument with eight metal strings

single–a song from an album that is used to help people find the album

solo–done alone

strums–moves fingers over the strings of a guitar

theme park–an amusement park where the rides or activities are based around a certain idea

To Learn More

AT THE LIBRARY

Heinrichs, Ann. *Tennessee*. Parker, Colo.: The Child's World, 2025.

Moening, Kate. *Dolly Parton: Country Music Star*. Minneapolis, Minn.: Bellwether Media, 2021.

Parton, Dolly. *Coat of Many Colors*. New York, N.Y.: Penguin Random House, 2016.

ON THE WEB

FACTSURFER

Factsurfer.com gives you a safe, fun way to find more information.

1. Go to www.factsurfer.com.

2. Enter "Dolly Parton" into the search box and click 🔍.

3. Select your book cover to see a list of related content.

BEYOND THE MISSION

> WHAT FACT FROM THE BOOK DID YOU THINK WAS THE MOST INTERESTING?

> WHAT QUESTIONS WOULD YOU ASK DOLLY ABOUT HER LIFE?

> WHAT DO YOU DREAM OF DOING WHEN YOU GROW UP?

Index